AF408317

FIRMAMENT

POEMS

CHRISTOPHER MARTIN

Wandering Aengus Press
Eastsound, WA

First Edition. Published by Wandering Aengus Press

Poetry
ISBN: 979-8-218-06307-8
Cover Art: Opal Martin
Book Design: Jill McCabe Johnson

Wandering Aengus Press
PO Box 334 Eastsound, WA 98245
wanderingaenguspress.com

Wandering Aengus Press is dedicated to publishing works to enrich lives and make the world a better place.

For my children always

———————————————

CONTENTS

II: SERPENT

III: Shade

All nature, all formations, all creatures
exist in and with each other. Everything
composed decomposes; everything returns
to its roots. All matter becomes its own origin.

—Gospel of Mary Magdalene

I: Mire

Marcescence

I hike a horse trail, tread moss and mud west of Kennesaw Mountain,
cross Noses Creek's crumbling banks. I stop, rest, sit on a rotting log
where stone piles of Confederate earthworks cover the ground,
testaments to what this place has seen, remnants of what it has been.
Here the woods are white, brittle with leaves still clinging to beech trees.
From a fallen beech, a hermit thrush murmurs, flutters farther into brush
when it sees me. Three whitetail does stand vigilant, in an instant vanish
through dusk, tails flared, one with trembling leaves these branches
will bear until spring, will bear as my own limbs hold whispers stirring,
these stories of what it means to die yet remain bound to a living thing.

Second Coming on South Cobb Drive

This great blue heron is in rebellion
of what I expect it should be.
It does not stand in grandeur;
rather, it crouches like a weary man,
waits in the water of a drainage ditch
filled with car parts, branches, beer cans,
beside a shack made of rims and road signs
nailed to rotting boards by South Cobb Drive.

Soon the heron lifts like a plastic bag
caught in an updraft, ascends over my car,
over the highway, one with exhaust and sky
set against Kennesaw Mountain, a ridgeline
eclipsing pawn shops, porn stores, fast food.
The great bird circles, settles among refuse
pooled at the mouth of the concrete stream,
watches the water for movement, for life,
as traffic slouches north.

Icarus at Allatoona

Waterlogged and barely floating
at the edge of Lake Allatoona,
a dead blue heron draws flies,
bobs in the wake of a distant boat.
Its wings expand in the sludge,
fill with the water beneath them,
spread over a body that rots
among cattails and reeds,
feeds creatures I cannot perceive.
From the bridge where I walk
with my children, the wingspan
appears out of place, worn
by some exiled angel, or a boy
who took flight only to fall,
drown in this lake, drift
to this inlet where nobody sees.
Pollen and sludge lap the feathers,
gather with bottles, plastic wrappers,
fishing line at the reservoir's edge.
Days from now, even these wings
will descend to silt, dissolve
within everything that remains,
recede with these relics, all this
artifice, these myths.

Feeding American Bison at the Yellow River Game Ranch

I lifted my son to my shoulders, held him
there beside a pen where we beheld bison
abiding in muck, lying among dead trees,
tires, woodpiles, boulders, and haybales,
the Yellow River's low-slung haze.

Recalling Job to whom God spoke, saying,
Behold now behemoth, this beast I made with you,
this monster of my ways only I may approach,
I watched a bison rise, shake off flies,
lurch the black earth our way; its eyes
and snout drained fluids that trickled
down the God-drawn lines of its face,
dripped from its beard like a spring.

It lumbered to the chain-link fence
where with muzzle and horns it shook
metal wires and waited, its mouth agape,
purple tongue unfurled, expecting food,
apples and crackers from the gift shop
where mass-produced dreamcatchers
webbed the antlers of mounted deer.

This beast that weathered cataclysm, endured
ever-long winters with mammoths, wildcats,
elk, herds of dappled horses, waited there
by the fence, for me and the child
on my shoulders, for us and anyone else
who would, to feed it, to approach it
such as we had and God said, once,
as he mocked a suffering man,
only he could do.

The bison licked sweet crumbs
from our palms. We were there, too,
then, those winters, abiding the ice,
the indifferent voice raging within
those whirlwinds. But we held on
to our children. I held on
to my child as I held
out my hand.

Lamentation by the Towaliga River

At a protest against the execution of Troy Davis

In Jackson, Georgia, on the banks
of the mist-laden Towaliga,

a man waits in a cell, sentenced
to die by poison needle.

We stand here for him.
We stand, crossed

by power lines,
beside a truck stop

on a hill by Highway 16
across which rises

a wall of riot gear,
paramilitary presence

among the pines.
Above, a helicopter churns,
drowns voices singing

This little light of mine,
drowns the light itself

filtering through
fractured woods.

In this place borne away
by the violent like blood

by the river,
I stand

watching children
reach for dragonflies.

My Grandfather Throws His Fishing Pole

Those months I lived with my grandparents,
he would still take me fishing, would still carry
that yellow rod and Zebco 33 reel he swore by,
tackle I'd associated with him since I was a boy,
though our tradition was beginning to fade.
I was older then, going on 14, had already seen
things I could not have known years before
standing beside him with my Looney Tunes pole,
fishing for bream with stale bread—
the rage bouts, the knives he pulled
from kitchen drawers during his arguments
with my grandmother, the cases
of cheap beer she kept in her closet
to make living with him a little less hard.

I had a Zebco rod and reel of my own by then,
the day I watched him tangle his line in a sweet gum,
curse the branches hovering just over the water,
hurl his pole in the pond when the line wouldn't loose.
He told me to keep fishing as he stomped off to his truck,
still cussing, so I stood there, wondering what to do,
whether I could save his pole. But it was too far out,
already sinking, a gleam of yellow beneath the green surface,
held from going completely under by that tangled line.

Not knowing what else to do—my grandfather
by then a lanky impression of flannel, ball cap, and blue jeans
disappearing across the earth dam between farm ponds—
I knelt down, scraped some nightcrawlers
from the pine straw, the loam beneath me,
threaded two on my hook. I cast my line
toward a shadow below those sweet gum limbs,
knowing that's where a big catfish would be—
the spot my grandfather had aimed for moments ago,
his pole now completely sunk, and that filament line
bending the thin branch, barely holding on.

A Privy on the Appalachian Trail

No amount of Imodium I carried
kept the curse from moving.
Call it *Still Life with Giardia*.
An image of a young man
hunched on a rickety toilet seat
mounted to an unroofed platform
in the southwest Virginia woods,
his Wal-Mart raincoat absorbing
sleet and rain like soil and duff
soaks up the diseased compost
he passes to the pit below.

Exposed, he shakes, bent
like the wild turkey he sees
brooding over loam in the cove,
early Appalachian spring dyed
silver by such weather, not a thing
untouched—red oaks, laurel, ferns,
polyester, toilet paper, human legs—
all of it sodden in the haze shrouding
the slopes of Hurricane Mountain.

Was it by some romance he drank
unfiltered creek water back in Georgia
when he started the trail, the same romance
by which I remember the icy cove silver?
It will pass, this romance, pass with the cold,
pass with the shit that has by now turned
to earth, earth that I, too, soon will be,
earth the young man I remember already is.

Jesus Year

I would've never believed, here and now at 33,
I'd be sitting in this rust-stained tub, soaking in vinegar
to relieve chigger bites speckling my legs, wounds
amassed the other night walking a meadow
along Allatoona Creek with my children.
Seeking barred owls and bats on a ranger-led hike,
we found none of the former, a few of the latter,
and plenty of what I never saw coming,
creatures inching along grass blades and weeds,
clinging to my leg hairs despite all precautions—
bug spray, tall socks, failed attempts
not to brush against the green, knowing
they were likely there, unseen. In my sleep,
they burrowed beneath my skin,
forced up the blisters that have led me here,
this day, to this acidic water, that have left me
worrying over all I did wrong on our walk,
over all I could've prevented,
all I might take from this pain
for the next time we go.

Narrow

He knows I don't know much about this machine,
this work, these cows that rush the fence,
force each other out of the way
as we approach in the tractor,
loader full of cornhusks to leave on the ground.
My father-in-law, something of a mother cow
to this herd—manifestation of sustenance, millet and hay—
drives, works gears, while I sit hunched in the cab,
my two children balanced on my lap.
He thinks I'm a city boy, and maybe I am.
He thinks I should lead my family and go to church.
I've never been sure he accepts who I am,
or that I've been a stay-at-home dad,
something he sees as feminine work,
a role meant for his daughter.
We draw nearer the pasture,
silent in this weight.
He asks me to open the gate.

Dog Star

Sirius rises late in the dark, liquid sky
on summer nights, star of stars,
Orion's dog, they call it, brightest
of all, but an evil portent bringing heat
and fevers to suffering humanity.
                    —The Iliad

July 4, 2018

In mosquito heat and ink sky,
we sweat, shift among bodies,
stop at a bridge we've crossed
countless times, this time to watch
fireworks erupt over a manufactured lake,
contrived as the spirit we wait for.
Our daughter sits on my shoulders,
our son on the bridge rail between us,
their innocence the only reason we've come.

All day we've spoken in whispers of Mexico,
of children no different from ours
but the color of their skin, the country
of their birth, of mothers, fathers
who have crossed deserts for them
all penned in centers flying flags
that tell our independence.

Today I'd sooner pledge my allegiance
to the stripes of the water snakes
that dwell in this lake, to the stars
that break suburban light and lit powder
exploding red, white, and blue around us.
I'd sooner pledge my life to the dog star
ignited above us, brighter than this spectacle,
though it holds a fire, carries a pain
these lights bursting in air only hide.

Revelation on the Cherokee County Line

At an exit ramp off I-75, a coyote rots, its body
green, not with fierce fire, but with fungus, mold
embalming its bloated remains, its once black hair.
Its face looks up from itself, a monster
petrified on concrete, teeth still bared.
Above this flesh, a sign says *Tourist Info*,
arrow points west, past the Wendy's.
What more information would they need
to tell them they are not here, but anywhere?

Battle Hymn: Highway 41, South

The radio preacher wails, spews
a litany: signs of the end times,
plain as the billboards overlooking
cars and freight reeling down 41
like crows in some vision of John.

He speaks of judgments—bowls, seals, trumpets—
that will answer our rebellion. He says a beast
will break from the sea, blood-soaked and wild,
to loom over water like these billboards that stand
in the swamps of Noonday Creek by which I drive,
through which other rebels once trudged
until they, too, were trampled like a vintage.

I cut the radio to better hear sirens howl,
brake as a fire truck flares by, lights gyring,
glaring in the gloam at the foot of Kennesaw,
a mountain resting in the sprawl, gray as a grave.

Gulf Fritillaries, Allatoona Creek

As we drove to this place, we noticed
more than one church sign that spoke of Satan.
NRA decals mocked a dead young man,
beckoned us to *Stand and Fight*.
A Confederate battle flag beat in wind
rushing a suburban lawn.
All this and every imaginable chain
asserted their names on this corridor
now split by 41, once by exile and war.

Whether this world is charged,
whether this is its time of flaming out,
are questions we cannot afford to ask here,
walking these trails through a county park,
ducking spider webs, tangles of muscadine,
stepping over logs and mud puddles,
watching our children wade, splash,
throw rocks in Allatoona Creek
where it runs along a sewer line.

In the clay sand, coyote scat marks this place
unknowable to us, not our own or anyone's,
draws a gathering of butterflies:

gulf fritillaries, alighting on excrement,
flaring flame wings in midmorning,
sucking the marrow of the waste,
consuming such redemption
as I have missed.

Parable of the Sandhill Cranes

Christmas morning, 2016

Incarnate words, sandhill cranes,
well over a hundred,
obscure the sun over Lake Allatoona,
trumpet the sky, their calls
creaking like an opening door.

If some have followed a star,
let us trail some sense
of direction, inborn and native,
more rooted than that which displaces us,
than those who offer no refuge here.

A truer country—
instinct woven in the mind,
collective remembrance—
waits beyond the interstate,
political boundaries,
imposition of lines.

Migrate, spirit: Become this flesh,
as flesh hovers with you
over these waters.

II: Serpent

Footnote to Genesis 3

It wasn't long
after the Fall
that the snake
brushed itself
against a pine
and shed its skin,
which a flycatcher
found and used
to line its nest,
to make itself
at home.

Conversion at Owl Creek

Last I was here, there was no blood,
only a sign, weathered and white.

Now, on our way to Brasstown Bald,
where Owl Creek Road pierces the wilderness,
I see the wood splattered red,
color concealing many letters,
its message the same:

> *The blood*
> *of Jesus Christ*
> *covers all sin.*

Whether the work of evangelists or vandals,
I do not know, but park beneath a white pine,
step to the sign, and, like Thomas, touch the wound
of paint, surprised to find it fresh.

Stooping among ferns, I submerge my hands,
wash the crimson in the creek, watch it diffuse
as it floats downstream, wait for it to disappear.

The Wish to Sing with Primitive Baptists

Northbound on Old 41, I pass a church
I've passed for years—Blue Springs Primitive Baptist,
resting between the highway and high school parking lot.

A board hangs out front, says *Singing tonight.*
I think how I'd like to join them, if I could, how I'd like
to take my son with me, now drifting to sleep
in his car seat behind me, how we'd both love
to sing if matters of belief were of no consequence.

It would come down to this, I know:
I do not believe in the resurrection of Christ,
in the sense that he just up and walked from the grave
only to ascend and wait to return for the world's last war.
I do not believe in the flame that, some say, awaits sinners,
unbelievers, doubters and seekers, followers of other faiths.
I do not believe in sin or salvation, in the righteousness of the chosen,
the fallenness of creation, the inherent corruption of the world.

I believe that God is going to sleep
in the seat behind me, and that is all.

They might tell me I am wrong, eventually, once they found out.
Even so, I imagine turning my car, waiting for the evening
song, for a thousand tongues to sing in communion
with this small congregation, a remnant people
in a remnant place, losing ground.

My Children Pile Sticks on a Headstone

Before the food, the barbecue and cobbler,
before the reunion beneath the shelter,
we must endure revival or wait outside for the sermon to end.
Every so often, the breeze eases enough that I can hear
the preacher droning inside Antioch Baptist,
a relic nearly overcome by woods off Duck Roost Road,
its windows smashed by vandals, white paint flaked, fading,
this the only day of the year it holds a congregation of anything
besides mice and wrens, paper wasps, surely occasional snakes.

Every so often, a stare cuts my direction through a broken pane;
every so often, the sad discussion of sin and death reaches
the cemetery, over a century old, where I sit with my children
as they gather sticks, start piling them on a headstone.

I stand, tell them *No, no, we can't put these here*, as I move the sticks,
my son waiting by the grave with more in his arms,
my daughter collecting those I've tossed aside,
ready to return them to the top of the stone.
At four and two, they don't know what this headstone means,
let alone what death is at all, and intend no disrespect,
despite looks shot through rock-shattered windows,
judgment trailing the sermon's echoes.

I brush the last of the sticks off the grave,
usher my children to the edge of the woods
where they touch moss, part muscadine vines,
draw pictures in the clay sand with sticks
they've carried from the cemetery.
Cicada song settles here, so thick
it drowns the last words of the sermon,
covers every word out of reach of this closeness.
I know nothing of death, either,
here, amid all this.

At Paradise Garden

For this world is not our lasting home; we seek a home that is to come.
        —Epistle to the Hebrews

Allatoona Range to Ridge and Valley,
Etowah River to the Oostanaula,
we drive two hours to Summerville,
cross Armuchee Creek, flank ridges
that saw Sherman make plans
to march to the sea, burn this all down.
Road cuts reveal seafloor rock—
age of the fishes, age of amphibians,
ancient time locked in highway embankments
of the Holocene—age of the atom bomb,
age of visions, age of the Word.

We turn off 27 before the Wal-Mart,
park in a ditch along a chain-link fence
where a scrap-metal-plated chapel—the World's
Folk Art Church—rises above a kudzu wall.
An obligatory photo by a cheap tarp sign—
R.E.M filmed their first music video here—
the chained dog barking from an adjacent yard,
the $10 entry at the gate, and we are in the festival.

Our daughter, age four, humors us a few minutes
before the irritability sets in, which not even a rainbow
snow cone soothes. I taste the ice as not to waste it—
frozen strawberry, lemon, grape, everything—
olive branch in the mouth of a makeshift dove,
nothing but cold sugar, not even bread,
which would not be enough in itself
to keep each tempter away.

I want to go home, she repeats several times
as concrete snakes, tricksters, prayer flags,
apocalyptic visions, and all the rest weave
like a serpent around us in this garden
pieced together by a man from another world.
The dust and garbage smell, the holy child,
holy mother, the shards of everything, signal
some fall, and a desire to absorb this place
and leave it all, to go home, which, after a while—
after so many mirrors, so much shattered
glass and trash transformed to art—is what we do.

Parable of the Flycatcher

My grandfather says the flycatcher
has yet to nest in the box by the garden
at the edge of the woods,
the bird whose song
is a whistling *weep*.

I show him my field guide, point to the bird
for which he waits—*Myiarchus crinitus*,
gray wings, pollen yellow belly,
bearing a grasshopper in its beak.

He considers the words on the page:

> *Nests in old woodpecker holes,*
> *but can be attracted to boxes…*
> *Often fills its nest with a collection of things:*
> *fur, feathers, string, and snakeskins…*

He says once he pulled
a snakeskin from the box
and it blew to dust
in his hand.

On this porch overlooking blossoming dogwoods,
the violent ghosts of my grandfather's past and my own
are at play in the trees, the scars of abuse and bloodshed
of the Korean War drifting in the breeze like kingsnake scales.

You know them birds, he says, *will use anything*
to build their nests. When I cut my hair,
I leave some for them in the grass.

Ringneck Snake

When asked, I emphasize the weight I've lost,
say nothing of how it really is sadness
that sends me running, some worry flooding
this skin, needing to seep with sweat,
some soreness I need to feel release.

I say nothing of thoughts of death
and the passing of things, thoughts
that assail and encompass all like this wind
moving in early winter, through which I move.

I say nothing of my children back home,
of how they stretch with me each time I leave,
of how they touch my cold hands and face
each time I return, of how each moment flees.

I say nothing of the ringneck snake
I saw lying nearly dormant on the concrete trail
by the cove at the end of a run. I say nothing
of the way the snake did not react to my presence
until I touched it, lifted it level to my beating chest
as it wove between my fingers,
wrapped around my wrist.

I say nothing of how I let it go,
watched it turn away to face another thing,
gold seam on its coal body disappearing
in weeds and leaf rot, finding shelter
in all the living and the dead
given to the understory.

Catching Salamanders at Indian Grave Gap

Following High Shoals Creek to Blue Hole Falls,
we stop for water, rest on rocks
where the trail splits a rhododendron hell,
descends farther into wilderness.
We've come as far as we will go,
my son and I, so we linger beside a cavern,
a wound in the mountain left by a fallen tree.
Roots reach from the earth-clods,
the lichen, the galax and ferns.
Shattered stones keep wet in the cut,
and we have not overturned three
before a salamander—black, back flecked
as the mica-strewn ground around us—
has emerged, crossed the mud beneath us.
I catch it, let it is slink from my hands to my son's,
his hands so small the salamander spans them
as it weaves between his fingers
before slipping away, returning to the radical.

As we hike back upstream, my son runs ahead,
points out white pine roots
that burst the earth, thread the trail before us.
He tells me they look like salamanders,
these roots slithering the woodland floor,
and asks me why they look that way.
Given this place's name,
I might've thought of human limbs,
burial, unearthed graves, desecration,
if I had thought anything at all.
But he's considered them more, these roots,
looked more closely at them, so I tell him
they match what's here,
leaving unsaid what he already knows:
That they mirror what moves unseen
below them, among the dark and decomposing,
what moves within this place and moment
that death does not touch.

Crawling Out of Christian Psychology

It was a Friday class, 7 am, three hours long,
one absence the loss of a letter grade.
I left my dorm those mornings in half-light,
groggy, though awake enough—
years before I'd need coffee—
and sulked with other students across campus
of the tiny Bible college in the mountains.
Back then, the Word meant something
different to me than it does now, seemed more vital
in that Christ-haunted lecture hall
where we gathered those Friday mornings.
I didn't mind the professor's opening prayers
or question the endless connection of everything
to the Bible—how sexuality squared with scripture,
Freud with Paul, how language squared with Babel,
human development with the Fall.

Still, nothing much held me in that moldy room
aside from grades, the threat of a lost letter
should I leave—not the professor's droning lectures,
the primordial projector slides,
the awkward silences of forced discussion—
and class ran through dining hall breakfast hours,
no assurance any food would be left once we were free.

So one morning, otherwise unremarkable,
after the professor opened with prayer, called roll,
marked me there, and turned to face the board,
carry on with class like each day before,
I slipped out of my seat near the back,
touched elbows to musty carpet,
slinked through aisles around my peers,
and crawled from Christian Psychology
like a fish crawling from the sea.

It's taken me years to find that metaphor,
though that morning, any significance was lost

on me: Then I believed the world as it is
was the world as it had always been,
that nothing much had ever changed,
that no fish had ever crept from the tide.
Back then, that morning, it was just too early,
and all I wanted was fresh air, daylight,
a little walk, a better chance of finding food.

Cyrene

At a meat-and-three in the foothills,
an old man walks table to table,
hands out crosses to children.

I've brought my children here to break the routine
of peanut butter and jelly lunches with soul food,
enjoy a meal, not so much wrestle with remnant faith
washed in shame, a faith I do not intend to pass down.

Eventually the man approaches our table,
says *Cute kids, I've got a present for them.*
I rush to swallow a mouthful of cornbread
and politely decline, but before I can, he's pulled
two small, metal crosses from his suit pocket,
extended them to my children, little boy and girl
who don't know what these symbols mean.
But the crosses are shiny, new,
and knickknack execution devices or not,
they lift them from the table,
study them, play with them,
slide them around dishes like toy cars.

Eventually both return to their food,
forget the gifts, do not notice as I move them
to my pockets—do not notice, once we leave,
as I drop their two crosses in the parking lot
and drive away, a heaviness on my back.

My Daughter Touches the Plutonium Square

We wander the museum's mineral wing,
pass petrified wood turned to quartz,
blinking maps illuminating
the mining zones of Georgia,
fluorescent rocks changing
colors at the push of a button.
My children touch everything
within reach, ignore my reading
of signs that say not to. They do
nothing different to the giant
periodic table covering the back wall:
My one-year-old daughter
slaps its glass case with all
she can muster, rests
a hand on a square far beneath
    the stable rows—
K, potassium signified by a banana,
Ca, calcium, by a seashell and cherry antacids.
    The actinides
are just her height, however, and soon she finds
Pu, taps a photograph, a mushroom cloud
bursting beside a note that explains
    plutonium, an element
Named after the planet Pluto,
used in nuclear weapons.
    I recall the smallness
of her hand within that frame,
the smallness
of any explanation.

Cutting Off Lithium

I only saw him on weekends then,
so maybe it was more about creating
silence so we could talk, father
to thirteen-year-old son.

He tolerated my music well enough,
though I don't think he understood
this song
was less about loud noise
and more testament to the ache
always lodged in my jaw, always
just shy of expression.

But that day, he might've been listening,
might've actually caught the lyrics—
whether it was the *I'm so horny*
or the *I killed you, I'm not gonna crack*
that pushed him to the edge,
made him cut the dial, I don't know.

Or maybe, since we were headed to church
when the song came on 99x,
it was the *Sunday morning
is every day for all I care*
that was the last straw.

Whatever it was, when we arrived
and he told me to tuck in my shirt
before we entered the sanctuary,
I think we both must have sensed
truth in the words that had been sung
and remained snagged in our silence.

Parable of the Kingfisher

Out of breath, I finish my run,
turn back on the lake trail toward home.
Years ago, I could've run both ways;
soon, perhaps, I will again, but for now
I'm content to walk, let my heart settle,
try to focus on nothing but my lungs taking air,
same that rushes through maples,
yellow leaves announcing their return to earth.

November dusk emerges on a zephyr,
weather not yet turned toward winter,
bears a warmth out of place, out of time.
A calm cradles the water, murmur
of gold beams interlacing the green lake.

Along a wooded cove, I stop,
realize I am alone. Across the lake,
golfers that seem small as crows from here
return to their carts, creep through pines
away from the green. Behind me, a siren
drones somewhere on Old 41, a sound
nearly hushed by a kingfisher's call.

I think of nothing and everything,
overcome by the kingfisher's laughter,
and strip to my boxers, bare
a body of which I'm often ashamed—
heavier, uglier than it once was,
traced by cheap tattoos I got at 19—
and wade into the cove's chill,
carrying worry like a stone.

Before me, trails of moonbeams catch fire,
refract in the fisher's wake as it skims the water
like a candle tracing twilight.
Weaving air and lake, the fisher
spirals along the tangled bank,
feet from where I swim, seeks fish
as I catch my breath and my body warms,
asks in its rattling cry
where my accusers have gone.

At the Etowah Mounds

We enter the ancient village by footbridge,
my son running ahead through a meadow
where butterflies and purple flowers bead the green,
my daughter bound to my hip, chomping a cracker,
crying every time I try to put her down.
A man with a weedeater crops grass below a mound
built by a people whose hush would fill a thousand years
were it not for these hills, the relics of culture
displaced in the wake of DeSoto and disease.

The machine whine stifles midmorning sounds—
birdsong, wind whistling in native grasses
planted by the DNR,
the whisper of the Etowah
making its way to Allatoona Dam.
We take a staircase up the side of Mound A,
rest on a bench at the top for a snack,
share lukewarm water from a plastic bottle.

The temple that once stood where we sit
binds itself now to a thing unknown,
as do the daub huts and cornfields
that filled the river valley
when a priest held this highest place
and two other mounds, almost as high,
housed the dead.

Today the only divination
pours from the coal plant due west in Euharlee,
smokestacks tracing skyline
like an invisible past, a thousand years gone,
still hardly anything figured out.

Tired of the bench and the stillness,
not troubled enough to take in the view,
my children tell me they're ready to go back down,
run the trail by the river, sit in a swing, see the geese.
I pack up the crackers and water,
pick up my daughter, hold my son's hand,
lead them back to lower ground.

III: SHADE

My Daughter Refuses to Smile

It's most often a man who demands it
when we're out, as it was in the grocery store aisle
one afternoon after I'd picked her up from school,
hauled her along on some errands.
Nothing at all wrong—a pleasant enough day,
low seventies, early spring.
But nothing, either, particularly warranting a smile,
except another day for life, breath,
thankfulness, joy, and all the rest,
though for that one might well smile forever.

I certainly don't recall smiling
as I scanned the cereal aisle,
grabbed a box on sale, tossed it in the buggy
beside my daughter. *Pretty little girl,*
the stranger said, passing by.
Wish she'd smile, though.

She didn't, of course, and if anything
her expression shifted
from one fully fitting minding one's own business
at a Kroger on a weekday afternoon,
to more of a glare—
her preschool perfection of an eat-shit-and-die stare—
and the only one left smiling was me.

My Son Covers His Ears in Church

*Truly I tell you, anyone who will not receive the kingdom of God like a little child
will never enter it.*
            —Gospel of Mark

He loves music more than any three-year-old I know—
treasures his own guitar, harmonica, even a banjo
he once took to a bluegrass concert to pick right along,
just about joining the band when they covered Steve Earle.
So it could not have been the music itself this morning
that made him cover his ears, cower in the pew,
ask to go outside when they finished the song.
Maybe he picked up on the lyrics' sad suggestion—
All I had to offer Him was brokenness and strife—
and wanted none of it, or maybe he thought the music
too loud, nearly shrill, for such a small space.
But more than likely he was just tired of sitting still,
surrounded by solemn ritual, and simply wanted
to go outside. Whatever his reason, I took him,
almost covering my ears, as well, to block such sounds
as insulted my soul, and we entered a kingdom
at the edge of a dirt road where we played an hour
until we stopped to rest in the shade,
waiting for those inside to return.

A Church Sign on Summers Street

Outside downtown Kennesaw, a church sign:
Jesus gave us life and transformation.
I look beyond it to the mountain, basking blue,
dark ink against dusk sky, ridge rising
from the electric glow of Highway 41,
lights of strip malls and suburban sprawl.
I say *rising*, though the mountain has risen
and now crumbles, as it has been crumbling,
transforming, for hundreds of millions of years,
born by orogeny long before the birth of Christ,
longer still before he came to haunt these hills.

Buzzards at Allatoona Pass

In droves, they drift thermals, char black
inscriptions burned on cumulus clouds—
more buzzards than I have ever seen
in one place, here where rails once cut
the Allatoona Range, straddled this ridge
where the Etowah River ceases, swells,
converges with riprap, converts to lake.

An elegy for pinewood banks become bone,
battlefield become burial ground, burial ground
become lake bottom, points of departure
become refuge for channel catfish among decay,

above water and wake of speedboats,
the buzzards float as they did in days
that stalked Atlanta's fall, before it rose,
morphed to mythical bird: days boys bled,
hundreds dead in mere hours, time kept
by wing beats, the somnolence of scavengers
marked upon sky like lost names upon stone.

Parable of the Hummingbird

Lantana flare, descending
into pink, green, and gold,
whirring the drive-thru,
carline-exhaust emerald,
metallic scales lighting
dollar fries: Tell me

what I should do. Tell me
what it is that separates us
other than this windshield.
Tell me and I will flee this truck,
drink this synthetic landscape with you.
Tell me in your flickering tongue,

churn in my chest, hum
We are freer than we believe.

A hundred-million years, fly:
Let my throat become ruby.
Let a fire catch inside me.
Let this drive become nothing,

this road nothing, this menu nothing,
this shopping center nothing, this work
nothing, this suburb nothing, this void
nothing. Soon you will leave

these mulched flowers, cross
the churchyard, drugstore, Dollar General,
Dallas-Acworth Highway, Confederate cemetery,
cross the Chattahoochee, Gulf of Mexico,
bound for the Caribbean, South America,
some wilder flower-covering come winter.

Yet pause with me here in New Hope, Georgia:
Give me some ember to hold, some green-scaled story.
Give me some memory of our creation
as the line moves and I fall back in.

Deer Crossing Old Mountain Road

From Little Kennesaw's flanks, night settled
upon woods, boulders cradled in darkness,
she steps to the roadside, stands illumined
by headlights, lowers her head, cowers there,
crosses, fearing me, wary of my presence.
I press the brakes, watch her black eyes flicker
in battery-lit lights. She lingers, gold grasses,
weeds, surrounding still hooves
at the edge of a mini-mansion yard.
She does not know what the armies bled for,
that armies converged upon this mountain
at all. Now she knows nothing but danger
of light not overcome by the darkness—
light beaming from my car, light from streetlamps.
She returns where the light does not endure.

Shady Dale Nirvana

Not long before we left the antebellum home
our mother was renting in Jasper County,
my sister gave me *Unplugged in New York*
on cassette tape for my birthday.
I played it for hours on a stereo
that sat on the heart pine floor of my room,
above a room Sherman once used as an infirmary
for his men on their march to the sea,
the room where our mother slept, cold
in divorce, in the drafts of a house
with more space than we needed
and the heavy breathing, eternal
sighing, of those sick soldiers,
so tired they could not sleep.

The music my sister gave me, hushed as it was,
kept me dancing faintly as moonlight
flickering in the pecan grove, beams wavering
like candles among derelict outbuildings, rumors
of little flames extinguished each morning.

Antidote to Narcissus

I've heard the great blue heron
cannot see its own reflection
cast from the water's surface—

a gift that it may never lose a fish
in the image of a perfect eye
or fail to see a frog amid
such slate feathers shed
from a rookery on high.

If only we could fade that way
into the mist of rivers,
into rhododendron shade;

if only we could be so beautiful
and not know a thing about it.

Parable of the Red-tailed Hawks

The preachers may say they believe
in angels in all their glory—
whose glory comes filtered of God—
and say they hear their holy songs above,
imagine wings of light and silver,
feathers of white unflawed.

And that is well and good:

But I wonder how one can speak
of angels, whose wings we have not seen,
when red-tailed hawks fly over interstates
on black-dappled, rust, red, white-brushed,
creation-colored wings,

and nest on rooftops
angels never would.

Sunset at Pigeon Hill

Something stills and settles here
at this boulder on Pigeon Hill,
though engines roil not far away
and traffic lights flare through oaks
like Federal fires. Exhaust smoke sweeps
woods and rocks where pine scent drifts;
above, wild geese bellow, elapse the light
reflecting from a waning moon that kindles
the Dead Angle, Cheatham Hill, the horizon.

A wren trills the memory
of shell-shattered trees;
a cardinal burns in bramble,
ember against green.

Already darkness descends.
Little Kennesaw's summit behind me,
I sit and wait for the shadow.

Psalm 139

He was overtired, battling the bedtime routine—
refusing his pajamas, kicking, running away
each time his mother tried to help him
step into his pants. Not an outright *fit*,
it was something more like resistance—
hearing but not listening, spirited and wild,
willed with some energy
wrought in the core of the earth.
I stepped in, told my son
there would be no bedtime story
if he didn't cooperate, a threat empty as the void
long before there was mass, matter,
long before bodies hurtled around suns.
Amid all this, he kept asking,
When you were little, where was I? Was I not here?
Mommy, when you were little, where was I?
We looked at each other, his mother and I,
unprepared for such sincere diversion.
She told him she'd answer his questions
when he put his pajamas on, but he kept
flailing, falling, careening the living room
like a chunk of primitive rock.
He asked the same questions several more times;
she kept saying she'd tell him once he listened.
But he never did, and for all that fight, once it faded,
he just went to bed in his underwear
without a story, without an answer
to where he was—where all his substance
was written, continually fashioned—
when as yet there were none of him.
We waited to hear heavy breathing
signal his sleep before we entered
his room's darkness, and quietly,
gently as we could, put his pajamas on.

My Daughter Laughs in Her Sleep

Near midnight, I sit at the computer
waiting for clothes to finish drying,
skimming an article on *the 10 proven ways
to deal with depression*, expecting nothing
but the normal procession of today to tomorrow:
I will fold the clothes, unplug cords,
cut the lights, lock the doors,
resisting the urge to check every closet,
to look beneath the couch, within each cabinet,
any place someone intent on harm might be hiding—
a secret bedtime routine of my childhood.

Over the dryer's thump, heat pumping against
a 20-degree night, wind rushing the vinyl siding,
I hear my daughter react to some vision,
giggle like she does when we play,
two-year-old girl who was not long ago
resisting sleep, as I at times resist waking.

Let me believe in whatever it was she just saw,
in whatever it was that danced through her mind
and she found to be funny, whatever jest,
whatever joy, dwells in her dreams,
whatever it is I so often forget
though it abides in darkness
just the other side of the wall.

Resurrection in a Battlefield below Kennesaw Mountain

If you've wandered here, waited, kept watch,
you've seen them: They are all that is green, shooting
forth from ground—man-of-the-earth, goldenrod, yarrow.
They are roots and fibers of roots. They are trees—
beech, oak, poplar, cedar, pine, all of them, each
pressed into bark, pitch, branch, and leaf.
They are that which propagates, springs,
and that which consumes springing—
loam, thistle, butterfly, flycatcher—
their blood forming, feeding, becoming
bodies again. They are alive and well, the dead
whose life streams veins of grass, this grass
shadowed by ochre, rust, gold-graced limbs
reaching from Kennesaw's slopes—this grass
my fingers sift for grasshoppers, my son wobbling
behind me, his hands parting grass, grass
at the forest edge hiding my wife, battlefield
grass her seat for breastfeeding our daughter.
To a gray-green blade, a grasshopper clings;
I catch it, kneel down, open cupped palms
before my son, and the dead
fly from flesh on blood-red wings.

My Children Gather Blue Jay Feathers

After our hike along the Etowah—
realm of the wolf spider and rat snake,
great blue heron and the muskrat—
we take the trail that circles the mounds,
earth shelters enfolding bone and spirit
resting with effigies traced in ochre,
treasures for the afterlife—
copper adornments, shells, feathers.

I lead the way as my children linger
picking honeysuckles that bloom, spill
from a defensive ditch, millennia old,
intact since the Mississippian.

I pass a pile of blue jay feathers,
some small scene of violence—spectral
indigo plumes tattered, flayed, caked in blood.
I don't point them out to my children,
though soon I turn to see they've found them
on their own, that they've stepped off the trail,
knelt in grass up to their waists,
to sort the feathers, sift dirt and leaves
for some sign of the bird.

What would descend from these skies,
slate over these red Allatoona hills—
hawk or spirit, something of both—
pin me to the ground,
rend and consume me here,
leave my remains
to refract such firmament light
flowering in the hands of children?

I reach out my hand
to you, whoever you are:
Take it in yours,
gather us up, hold us near,
but let us abide ever here.

Acknowledgments

My gratitude to Jill McCabe Johnson, Tina Schumann, and the editors of Wandering Aengus Press, as well as to the editors and publishers of the following journals, anthologies, chapbooks, and other media in which many of the preceding poems appeared, sometimes in different form:

Bridge Eight • *Broad River Review* • *Buddhist Poetry Review* • *Fourth River* • *Loose Change* • *Menacing Hedge* • *museum of americana* • *New Southerner* • *Poecology* • *Red Clay Review* • *Ruminate* • *Sanctuary* • *Share* • *Still: The Journal* • *St. Sebastian Review: A Queer Christian Literary Magazine* • *Sugar Mule* • *Town Creek Poetry* • *Thrush*

Stone, River, Sky: An Anthology of Georgia Poems (Negative Capability Press, 2015)

The World is Charged: Poetic Engagements with Gerard Manley Hopkins (Oxford UP/Clemson UP, 2016)

The Southern Poetry Anthology, Volume V: Georgia (Texas Review Press, 2012)

Marcescence: Poems from Gahneesah, co-authored with David King (Finishing Line Press, 2014)

Everything Turns Away (La Vita Poetica Press, 2014)

A Conference of Birds (New Native Press, 2012)

"Marcescence" was first published as a broadside by Thrush Press.

"My Children Pile Sticks on a Headstone," "The Wish to Sing with Primitive Baptists," "My Daughter Laughs in Her Sleep," and "At the Etowah Mounds" appeared as transitional section breaks in my essay collection *This Gladdening Light* (Mercer UP, 2017).

My gratitude also to everyone—family, friends, teachers, students, and fellow writers—who have contributed to what this book has become. A special thanks to those associated with Kennesaw State MAPW and the Appalachian Young Writers Workshop.

About the Author

Christopher Martin is author of the essay collection THIS GLADDENING LIGHT, for which he received the Georgia Author of the Year Award in Memoir and the Will D. Campbell Award in Creative Nonfiction. *Firmament* is his first poetry collection. [www.chrbrmartin.com]

Winners of the Wandering Aengus Book Award

Marcia Aldrich: Studio of the Voice

Lucy Ferriss: Meditations for a New Century

Steven Harvey: The Beloved Republic

Amanda Hawkins: When I Say the Bones, I Mean the Bones

Christopher Martin: Firmament

Kevin Miller: Vanish

Michael Schmeltzer: Empire of Surrender

Alina Ştefănescu: dôr

Tarn Wilson: In Praise of Inadequate Gifts